Test Your Professional English

Finance

Simon Sweeney

Series Editor: Nick Brieger

6163

D1460485

To Judith, Ruth and Neil, with love from Dad.

Pearson Education Limited
Edinburgh Gate
Harlow
Essex CM20 2JE, England
and Associated Companies throughout the world.

ISBN 978-0-582-45160-5

First published 1997 under the title *Test Your Business English: Finance*
This edition published 2002
Text copyright © Simon Sweeney 1997, 2002
Fifth impression 2007

Designed and typeset by Pantek Arts Ltd, Maidstone, Kent
Test Your format devised by Peter Watcyn-Jones
Illustrations by Anthony Seldon
Printed in China
EPC/05

Acknowledgements
The author would like to thank Philip Cropper and Adrian Quin of Brewin Dolphin Securities for their help with some key terms and Simon Blackley for help with source material. Thanks to colleagues and friends in the School of Management, Community and Communication at the College of York St John. Thanks too, to the series editor Nick Brieger and to Helen Parker and Jane Durkin of Penguin Longman. Lastly, thanks to Iain Bain for final editing of the manuscript.

Published by Pearson Education Limited in association with Penguin Books Ltd, both companies being subsidiaries of Pearson plc.

For a complete list of the titles available from Penguin English please visit our website at www.penguinenglish.com, or write to your local Pearson Education office or to: Penguin English Marketing Department, Pearson Education, Edinburgh Gate, Harlow, Essex CM20 2JE.

Contents

Section 6: Investing your money

Section 7: Companies and the business environment

Section 8: The economic environment

To the student

Do you use English in your work or in your studies? Maybe you are already working in business, perhaps in a finance department, or in a finance organization. Or perhaps you are a student doing a business studies course. If you need to improve your knowledge of finance and financial terms in English, this book will help you. You can check your knowledge of basic finance concepts, key words and essential expressions so that you can communicate more effectively and confidently in your work and for your studies.

There are eight sections in the book. The first section is an introduction to general finance terms and concepts. The remaining seven sections each cover a different area of finance from planning to looking after investments. The book covers not only managing company finances, but also other aspects such as personal investments and the wider international environment. You can either work through the book from beginning to end or select tests according to your interests and needs.

Many tests also have useful tips (advice) on language learning or further professional information. Read the tips: they offer important extra help.

Many different kinds of tests are used, including sentence transformation, gap-filling, word families, multiple choice, crosswords and short reading texts. There is a key at the back of the book so that you can check your answers; and a word list to help you revise key vocabulary.

Your vocabulary is an essential resource for effective communication. The more words you know, the more meanings you can express. This book will help you develop your specialist financial vocabulary still further. Using the tests you can check what you know and also learn new concepts and new words, all related to finance, in a clearly structured framework.

Simon Sweeney

The full series consists of:

Test Your Professional English: Accounting	Alison Pohl
Test Your Professional English: Business General	Steve Flinders
Test Your Professional English: Business Intermediate	Steve Flinders
Test Your Professional English: Finance	Simon Sweeney
Test Your Professional English: Hotel and Catering	Alison Pohl
Test Your Professional English: Law	Nick Brieger
Test Your Professional English: Management	Simon Sweeney
Test Your Professional English: Marketing	Simon Sweeney
Test Your Professional English: Medical	Alison Pohl
Test Your Professional English: Secretarial	Alison Pohl

1 Who's who in finance

Match each job title on the left with the correct definition on the right (a–j). Use the grid below.

1 tax inspector	**a** The person who is responsible for an individual bank.
2 tax consultant	**b** Someone who advises people on how to manage their financial affairs.
3 bank manager	**c** Someone who prepares an individual's (or a company's) tax return.
4 commodity trader	**d** The person who is responsible for the financial side of running a business.
5 accountant	**e** A government official who checks that you are paying enough tax.
6 finance director	**f** The person who finds you the best insurance policy at the best price.
7 market analyst	**g** Someone who buys and sells stocks and shares for clients, and charges a commission.
8 financial advisor	**h** Someone who advises you or a company on how to pay less tax.
9 insurance broker	**i** Someone who comments on business and share prices in a particular sector of the economy.
10 stockbroker	**j** Someone who buys and sells large quantities of goods, especially food products such as tea, coffee, and cereals, or raw materials such as wood, or metals.

1	2	3	4	5	6	7	8	9	10
e									

 The word ending *-or* or *-er* indicates someone who does something. In many cases there is a related verb: *inspector* (*inspect*), *manager* (*manage*), *trader* (*trade*), *director* (*direct*), *advisor* (*advise*).

2 What's what in finance

Match each word on the left with the correct definition on the right (a–o). Use the grid below.

1	pension	a	Something that the government collects and no one likes to pay.
2	bank	b	Where you go to borrow money or get cash.
3	tax	c	How you are charged for borrowing money.
4	dividends	d	How you can pay for a house, unless you can pay for it in a single payment.
5	shares	e	A type of investment made by a company when buying equipment.
6	inflation	f	What, in financial terms, a business hopes to make.
7	bankruptcy	g	What a company has to prepare every year for presentation to its owners and to the relevant authorities.
8	capital spending	h	The situation where a company does not have enough money or property to pay its debts, and so the company closes.
9	profit	i	The total amount of sales in a year.
10	interest	j	Rising prices, rising costs and rising wages in an economy.
11	assets	k	What you buy if you invest money in a company.
12	turnover	l	Individuals who invest their money in a company hope to receive these regularly.
13	liabilities	m	When you are old, you hope to have one of these.
14	accounts	n	The name for all the property, equipment, investments and money owned by a company (or individual).
15	mortgage	o	The name for everything that a company owes.

1	2	3	4	5	6	7	8	9	10	11	12	13	14	15
m														

Make a new sentence for each of these terms, either about yourself, or about your company.

3 Word families

Financial vocabulary covers several areas, including economics, banking, marketing, personal finance and financial planning. Here is a selection of key words. Complete the table.

	Verb	Personal noun	General noun	Adjective
1	to analyze			
2		competitor		
3			advice	
4	to merge	–		
5	to industrialize			
6		trader		
7				exporting/ exported
8		producer		
9		supplier		
10		consumer		
11	to guarantee			
12	to credit			
13			debit	
14		earner		
15		investor		

4 Pictures used in talking about finance

Pictures often help to make information clearer. This test introduces language used to describe pictures of financial data. Match the words below with the correct numbers in the pictures.

---

broken line   column   curve   dotted line   fluctuating line

histogram/bar graph   horizontal axis   line graph   pie chart   row

segment   solid line   ~~table~~   undulating line   vertical axis

---

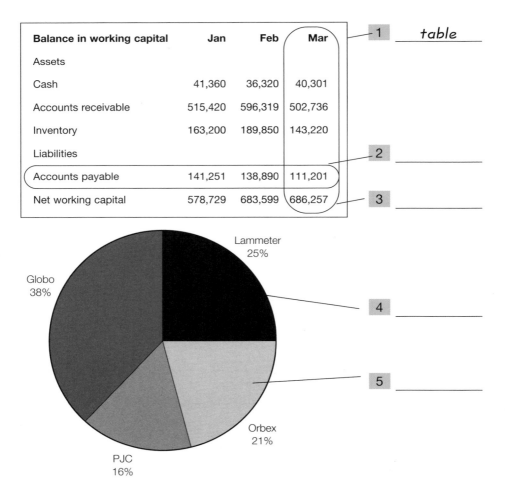

Balance in working capital	Jan	Feb	Mar
Assets			
Cash	41,360	36,320	40,301
Accounts receivable	515,420	596,319	502,736
Inventory	163,200	189,850	143,220
Liabilities			
Accounts payable	141,251	138,890	111,201
Net working capital	578,729	683,599	686,257

1 *table*

2 _____

3 _____

Lammeter 25%

Globo 38%

Orbex 21%

PJC 16%

4 _____

5 _____

6 ______________

7 ______________

8 ______________

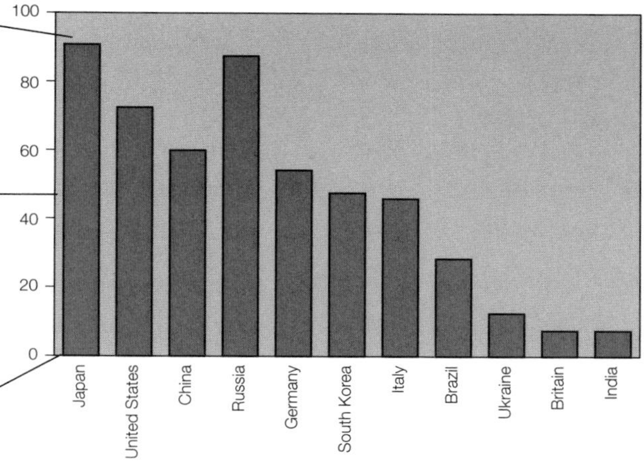
100
80
60
40
20
0
Japan
United States
China
Russia
Germany
South Korea
Italy
Brazil
Ukraine
Britain
India

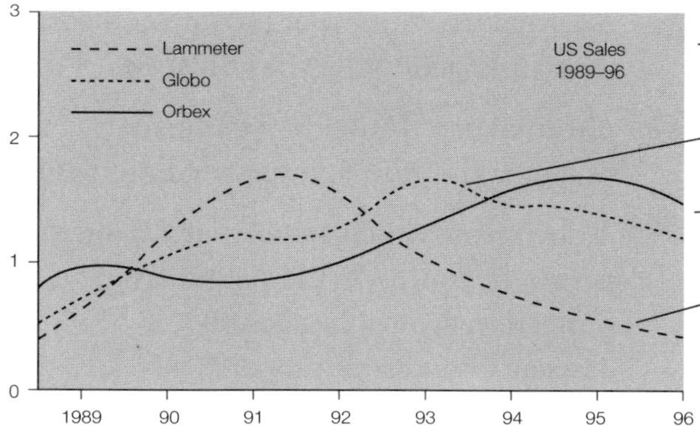
Lammeter
Globo
Orbex
US Sales
1989–96
3
2
1
0
1989
90
91
92
93
94
95
96

9 ______________

10 ______________

11 ______________

12 ______________

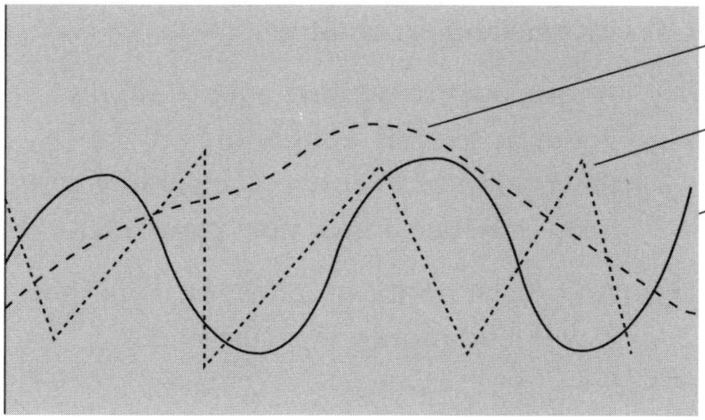

13 ______________

14 ______________

15 ______________

Accounts receivable means money that the business receives (income).
Accounts payable means money that the business pays out (costs).

5 Financial documents

Match each word on the left with the correct definition on the right (a-i). Use the grid below.

| 1 | profit and loss account | a | A plan of cash income and cash spending for a specific period of time. |

1 profit and loss account

a A plan of cash income and cash spending for a specific period of time.

2 balance sheet

b A document which represents a part of the total stock value of a company and which shows who owns it.

3 cash budget

c A formal agreement for the exchange of goods or services in return for payment.

4 share certificate

d A formal description of income and costs for a time period that has finished.

5 tender

e A formal description of a company's financial position at a specified moment.

6 business plan

f A document which states that a named person or company has paid for protection against accidental loss or damage of goods or property.

7 insurance certificate

g A description of the ways a new business hopes to make money, showing possible income and expenditure.

8 letter of credit

h A formal letter with an offer to supply goods or services, containing a description of the project, including costs, materials, personnel, time plans, etc.

9 contract

i An official notification from a bank that it will lend money to a customer.

1	2	3	4	5	6	7	8	9
d								

6 Describing trends

There are many ways to describe change. This test looks at several alternatives.

A Choose words from the box which are the opposite to each of the following words.

> decline   decrease   escalate   expand   ~~fall~~
> get worse   go down   improve   peak

rise/ ___fall___   increase/ _____   go up/ _____

climb/ _____   shrink/ _____   deteriorate/ _____

get better/ _____   collapse/ _____   hit bottom/ _____

B Match each word or phrase (1–9) to one of the graphs below (a–i). Look at the line between the two crosses.

1	decline to nothing	6	recover
2	collapse	7	increase steadily
3	stay the same	8	fluctuate
4	reach a peak	9	rise slightly
5	edge down		

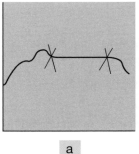

a

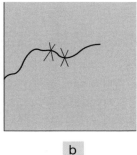

b

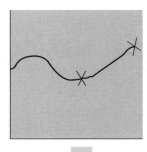

c

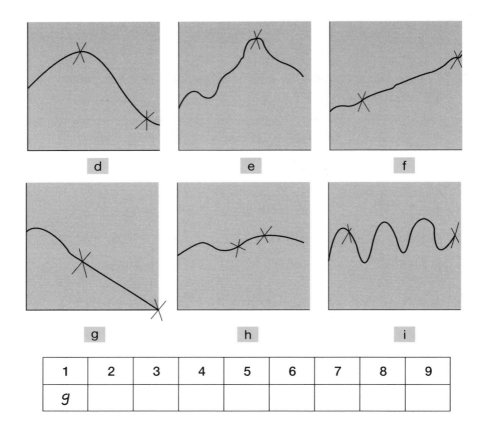

| d | e | f |
| g | h | i |

1	2	3	4	5	6	7	8	9
g								

 Notice the use of prepositions after verbs to indicate trends, e.g. *increase, rise, go up, decrease, fall, drop, go down*.

- increase *by* more than 20 per cent the remuneration payable (difference)
- increase *to* £40,000 the remuneration payable (final level)

Note: **remuneration** means financial reward, or payment, e.g. **remuneration package**. A remuneration package may consist of a basic salary plus various **perks** (additional rewards) such as accommodation, car, insurance, holidays, transport costs, etc.

7 Types of company

There are five main types of legally constituted company. Each type of company has different characteristics. Tick the correct characteristics for each business type, or write 'possibly' if the characteristic could apply.

	Public Limited Company	Private Limited Company	Sole Trader	Partner-ship	Co-operative
Single individual owns company			✓		
Two or more owners/ directors					
Quoted on stock exchange					
Workers run the company					
Unlimited liability					
Limited liability					
Owner is self-employed					

8 Common abbreviations

What do the following abbreviations mean? Fill in the missing letters.

1	VAT	Value A _dded_ T_a_x
2	PLC	Public L _ _ _ _ _ _ C _ _ _ _ _ _
3	Ltd	L _ _ _ _ _ _
4	& Co.	_ _ _ _ _ _ _ _ _ y
5	CWO	C _ _ _ W _ _ _ Order
6	COD	Cash O _ D _ _ _ _ _ _ _
7	c.i.f	c _ _ _ , i _ _ _ _ _ _ _ _ , freight
8	PAYE	Pay A _ Y _ _ E _ _ _ (i.e. tax)
9	p/e ratio	p _ _ _ _ /earnings r _ _ _ _
10	P & L account.	P _ _ _ _ _ and L _ _ _ account

COD can be a fishy business

COD means cash on delivery, and *cod* is a common type of fish (its Latin name is *gadus morrhua*).

A **fishy business** means not exactly legal, for example an attempt to avoid paying tax.

9 Introducing key terms in financial planning

Complete the sentences below with a word from the box.

> break-even point   core activity   cost of sales   gross profit margin
> net profit margin   overheads   ~~profitability~~   selling costs
> setting-up costs   turnover

1   *profitability* shows how a business might make profits. It is calculated from the relationship between profit and the capital invested in the company, and between profit and turnover.

2   The _____ of a business is the total amount of sales, before costs are deducted.

3   The _____ of a business is the main product or service which the business provides, e.g. for FIAT it is cars.

4   The _____ is the profit the business makes before costs are considered.

5   The _____ are the costs involved in creating a new business.

6   The _____ are the normal costs of a business, which do not change if production rises. They are also referred to as indirect costs or fixed costs.

7   The _____ is a calculation of profit after deducting the cost of sales and overheads.

8   The _____ are all the costs directly associated with producing the products.

9   The _____ is the amount of sales a company needs to cover all costs.

10   The _____ are all costs directly concerned with getting customers to buy products and moving them to the customer.

Noun + noun combinations are common in English. The first noun qualifies the second one. Examples are *London University, sales costs, setting-up costs, software company*.

10 Costs? What costs?

Put the terms in the box under the correct heading, then match them to the correct picture (1–7).

| administrative costs | advertising costs | distribution costs |
| ~~labour costs~~ production costs | selling costs | storage costs |

Fixed costs	Variable costs
labour costs (2)	

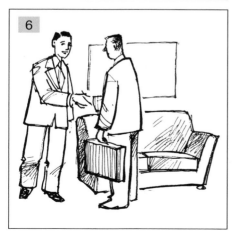

11 Identifying costs

Costs offer all businesses a major challenge. Good cost control is essential.

Read the definitions below, then complete the phrases that follow by combining an appropriate word from the box with *cost(s)*.

| analysis | centre | ~~fixed~~ | labour | manufacturing |
| operating | price | sales | selling | variable |

1. Usual expenses such as rent, heating, lighting, which are not changed by the volume of production. ___*fixed*___ costs

2. Expenses which increase with increased production, e.g. labour, raw materials. _____ costs

3. All costs directly related to production. _____ costs

4. All costs directly related to getting someone to buy a product. _____ costs

5. The cost of employing workers and staff. _____ costs

6. The costs for the day-to-day running of a company or business. _____ costs

7. Selling at a price which is exactly what the product has cost to make. cost _____

8. The study of all likely costs associated with a product. cost _____

9. A business in a chain, or a subsidiary, but treated as independent for accounting. cost _____

10. The total costs for all products sold. cost of _____

12 What's a master budget?

A Here is part of a description of a master budget, given in a class to management trainees. Complete the spaces with appropriate words from the box.

administrative   budget   capital   cash   fixed   forecast
~~income~~   raw   sheet   turnover   variable

In business planning, a company financial controller needs to prepare a master budget. This is a budgeted (1) _income_ statement which shows (2) _____ income and expenditure, and also a balance (3) _____ .

The master budget summarizes various forecasts, or budgets. Each of the following needs its own (4) _____ : sales, showing expected (5) _____ , production, showing all overheads and costs, both (6) _____ and (7) _____ , e.g. labour, (8) _____ materials and components.

A separate (9) _____ expenditure budget shows major spending on equipment and machinery. Another budget shows all general and (10) _____ expenditure that the business needs. Also, a (11) _____ budget shows estimated income and expenditure of cash, i.e. not cheque or credit card payments or payments by banker's order.

B Find words in the above text which mean the same as the following.

a	estimated	b	investment
c	revenue	d	spending
e	income and expenditure plan		
f	a regular payment to a creditor's bank account, where the creditor can change the amounts paid		

- **Sales, income, receivables** and **revenue** all indicate money received. **Costs, liabilities, expenditure, outgoings, overheads, payments,** and **expenses** all indicate money paid out.

- **Turnover** refers to total money received for all goods and services, sometimes referred to as **invoiced sales**. The **invoice** is, of course, the document which records the sale and requests payment. The word *turnover* is also used in the phrase **staff turnover**, to indicate the extent to which employees leave the company and are replaced.

13 Cash terms

Read the definitions below, then complete the phrases that follow by combining an appropriate word from the box with *cash*.

advance	budget	delivery	flow	hard	~~petty~~
	price	ready	settlement		

1. Small amounts of money in notes and coins for regular, small purchases. _**petty**_ cash

2. Money in notes and coins, not cheques or credit card transfers. _____ cash

3. Cash which comes in to a company from sales, after costs, overheads, etc. cash _____

4. Payment when the customer receives the goods. cash on _____

5. Plan of cash income and expenditure. cash _____

6. A loan in cash against a future payment. cash _____

7. Notes and coins available for immediate expenditure. _____ cash

8. Payment of a bill with cash. cash _____

9. A low price for payment in cash. cash _____

14 Sales forecasting

Sales forecasting is based on a variety of estimates, depending on the product or service concerned and the market involved.

A Below is part of a report by Michelle Cardot, the Marketing Manager of Fastrail Ltd, an urban transport system operator. Put the five parts of the report in the correct order.

1 The sales forecaster interviews sales staff, sales managers and senior management. Talking with experts and analyzing figures from previous years helps to show trends, the relationship between price and demand, and any seasonal variations. The forecaster also considers the effects of advertising, or changes in the market. For example, if new competition arrives or old competitors disappear.

2 **4.2 Sales forecasting**

Sales forecasting is an attempt to estimate the level of regular business. It includes existing contracts, the typical volume of sales to regular customers, typical volume of non-regular business and an estimate of the volume of new business.

3 Sales volume will be affected by the effectiveness of advertising and other promotional activities, the quality of the sales force, past sales volume and any seasonal influences.

4 Pricing policy is affected by market conditions, competition, economic climate, industrial conditions and organizational cost structure.

5 Factors affecting sales forecasting include pricing policy and sales volume.

Report

2 ☐ ☐ ☐ ☐

B Here is a memo based on the same report. Put the five sections of the memo into the correct order.

1
Factors affecting pricing policy:
market conditions, competition, economic climate, industrial conditions and organizational cost structure.

2
Forecasting uses personal interviews with both staff and management and also analysis of past sales figures. The relationship between price and demand can also be significant.
   At all times, forecasts can be adjusted, depending on changes.

3
Factors affecting sales volume:
advertising, promotional activities, quality of sales force, past sales volume and seasonal variation.

4
Fastrail Ltd
REPORT
From: Michelle Cardot – Marketing Director
To: JT, DS, HR, PD, PV
Date: 22 October 2002
Subject: Sales forecasting

Sales forecasting estimates the level of future business, combining volume of sales to regular customers with non-regular business and probable demand from new business.

5
Factors affecting sales forecasting:
pricing policy and sales volume.

Memo

☐ ☐ ☐ ☐ ☐

Notice the format for writing dates: 22nd October 2002 or 22 October 2002. However, when speaking, we say: the 22nd of October. In American English the month usually comes before the day, e.g. October 22, 2002.

15 Price–demand relationship

Find words or phrases in the text which mean more or less the same as the phrases given.

The Crown slips – US truck giant drops top seller

FD Auto, the largest independent truck manufacturer in the USA, yesterday announced plans to end production of its biggest-selling truck, the Crown 5000. Over half a million Crown trucks have been sold in 20 years, but sales in the past five years have declined to only 9,000 last year.

Three years ago the company cut prices by 20% to try to stimulate demand but sales rose by less than 5%. The price cut ate up the entire margin. Even in the normally price-sensitive US truck market, the Crown could not recover.

'It's a sad day, but we have to face reality. The Crown has passed its sell-by-date,' said Laurie Seller, the Marketing Manager for FD Auto. He accepted that the price cut had failed, saying that the company had miscalculated. 'Demand for the Crown is now totally inelastic: price does not affect demand. It's a dead truck. We cannot make any profit.'

It is not all bad news for FD Auto, however. Annual sales showed a small increase and turnover is expected to rise in the components division.

1 consumers wanting to buy the product

2 difference between cost price and selling price

3 easily influenced by price changes

4 is old-fashioned

5 reduction in price

6 not affected by price changes

7 sales in a year

8 total sales

16 Key terms in managing company finances

A Match the phrases on the left with a word or phrase on the right which means the same.

1	contribution ratio		a	turnover
2	fixed costs		b	gross profit margin
3	variable costs		c	overheads
4	income from sales		d	direct costs

B Match the term on the left with an appropriate definition on the right.

1	contribution		a	The number or total value of sales necessary to equal all costs.
2	capital costs		b	An individual cost centre in a company's product range.
3	gearing		c	Net profit available for reinvestment in the company.
4	retained profit		d	Sales income less variable costs.
5	work-in-progress		e	Selling price less variable costs divided by volume of production.
6	wealth		f	Cost of buying fixed assets such as buildings, equipment, vehicles.
7	unit contribution		g	Relationship between the cost of borrowing money and the total equity capital.
8	break-even point		h	Work done which has cost the company but has not yet been sold.
9	strategic business unit		i	Net value of a company (total assets less total liabilities).

1	2	3	4	5	6	7	8	9
d								

17 Setting up a business

Look at the four formulae below and then complete the spaces in the conversation below.

Contribution = sales revenue – variable costs

Profit = Total value of contributions – total costs; or

Profit = Revenue – {variable costs + fixed costs}

Break-even volume of production = $\dfrac{\text{fixed costs}}{\text{unit contribution}}$

Teacher: All products sold should make a contribution to the business.

Student: What is contribution?

Teacher: It is the total selling price of all goods sold by the company, (1) ___*sales*___ ___*revenue*___ , less (2) _____ _____ .

Student: So, it's like margin.

Teacher: Yes, it's the same as the gross profit margin. But, to calculate profit, you have to consider (3) _____ costs. In other words, the total value of contributions less (4) _____ and (5) _____ costs.

Student: I see. And when you've made enough contributions, you reach your break-even point.

Teacher: Yes, that's right. Then you start to make profit.

Student: How do you calculate the break-even point?

Teacher: You have to divide the (6) _____ _____ by the (7) _____ _____ or the contribution made by a single item that you sell.

Student: So if you raise your price, you increase the value of the contributions.

Teacher: Yes, but you must not raise your price so much that you lose sales. If demand is (8) _____ , sales may fall.

18 Overheads

Here is a list of 16 fixed cost items. Categorize them according to the headings given below.

accountancy fees	leasing of computers
books, newspapers	mortgage payments
car and van hire	professional indemnity insurance
car hire purchase agreements	rent
~~electricity account~~	salaries
employee National Insurance contributions	secretarial support
employer's liability insurance	stationery and printing
equipment, machinery	telephone

Services

electricity account

_____

Employee costs

_____

_____

Insurance

_____

_____

Administration

_____

Property

_____

_____

Professional fees

_____

Vehicles

_____

_____

Equipment

_____

_____

Miscellaneous costs

_____

_____

Miscellaneous means anything that does not fit easily into any of the given categories. **Miscellaneous costs**, therefore, are any other costs not already mentioned.

19 Cashflow problems and other difficulties

Choose the correct definition for each of the terms in italics.

1 *cashflow*

a) money from sales and money going out to meet costs, both fixed and variable

b) cash available to pay debts

c) payment of fixed costs, including salaries

2 *to reschedule overdraft payments*

a) stop paying overdraft credits to the bank

b) set a new level of payments and/or change the frequency of payments to the bank

c) ask the bank for a bigger loan

3 *liquidity problem*

a) not paying debts

b) customers who are late in making payments

c) not enough cash available to pay for costs

4 *liquid assets*

a) wealth that can easily be changed into cash

b) property that cannot be easily changed into cash

c) stocks and shares in drinks companies

5 *bad debts*

a) large bills to pay

b) old invoices that the customer has not paid

c) customers who always pay late

6 *to go into liquidation*

   a) to have a lot of money, especially cash

   b) to go bankrupt and to stop trading

   c) to be taken over by another company

7 *to record a credit deficit*

   a) to have no profits

   b) to be refused credit by a supplier

   c) to make a loss

8 *debit balance*

   a) the same as a credit deficit

   b) debits and credits are equal

   c) the number of debits is the same as the company forecast

9 *capacity problem*

   a) workers are not able to meet production needs

   b) the company is already producing the maximum quantity
       possible, but there is demand for more

   c) costs are at the maximum level the company can afford and
       the bank will not lend any more money

10 *opportunity cost*

   a) the costs associated with doing new business

   b) the cost of not doing something

   c) the cost of research and development

20 Financial control

Businesses have to work out the most efficient ways to produce products and services at a profit. This test introduces some key terms for this aspect of managing company finances. Match the term on the left to the correct definition on the right.

Financial planning term

1	profitability
2	return on investment (ROI)
3	liquidity
4	leverage
5	break-even point (BEP)
6	efficiency

Definition

a	the amount of products or services a company needs to sell to cover all its costs
b	ratio of total debts to total assets
c	measure of profitability obtained from dividing net income by total amount invested
d	ratio of total sales to total cost of inventory (goods in storage)
e	ratio of cost to benefit
f	measure of how well a business can meet its short term cash needs

1	2	3	4	5	6
e					

A key function in financial planning is to keep control of **investments** (spending). All the terms in this test are important in ensuring the efficiency of a business. Good planning often means making separate calculations and judgements for different activities in the same business. In this way, profitable units can be further developed. Weak units can be changed or abandoned. The correct term for these units is **strategic business unit** (SBU). A company treats each separate SBU as an individual **cost centre**.

21 Working out the break-even point

Look at the diagram below showing the break-even point for a business. Then complete the description below using words from the box.

break-even point   ~~fixed costs~~   loss   profit   sales revenue   total costs   variable costs

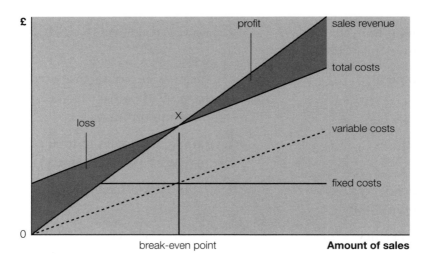

The horizontal line shows (1) __fixed costs__ . The dotted line which starts at point 0 shows the (2) _____ for different levels of sales. The (3) _____ are fixed costs and variable costs combined. The solid line starting at point 0 shows the (4) _____ at different levels of units sold. Point X is the (5) _____ . To the left of point X, the business is making a (6) _____ . To the right, the business is in (7) _____ .

22 If the price is right ...

In an interview with a journalist, Jan Horst, a marketing consultant, speaks about pricing policies. Complete the text of the interview with words or phrases from the box.

competition   cost plus   discount   ~~margin~~   marginal cost
market price   penetration strategy   skimming strategy

Journalist: So, in terms of pricing, what mistakes do small companies often make?

Horst: They take the cost of sales, and add to it – inventing a
(1) ____*margin*____ . This is a (2) _____
_____ approach.

Journalist: What's the alternative?

Horst: First, fix a price somewhere near or below the competition,
the (3) _____ _____. This can get you
market share, using a so-called (4) _____
_____ .

Journalist: What about (5) _____ _____ , just a
bit above variable costs?

Horst: Marginal cost pricing only works if you have a lot of spare
stock. It can help with a (6) _____ policy.

Journalist: And how can pricing help to build up market share?

Horst: First, a low price is essential to build up market share in
many markets. This is the penetration strategy approach. Or
you can have a (7) _____ _____ ,
with high margins to help to pay costs quickly. This is often
used with hi-tech goods. They start expensive but prices
come down quickly once the (8) _____ arrives.

23 Operations control

A key aspect of managing company finances is keeping control of operations. Operations means all aspects of organizational activity. Read the text below, then match the underlined phrases to one of the terms in the box.

Operational control brings financial rewards

Many businesses and organizations have a 1) <u>strategic approach</u> to management. Good operational control is essential. One important tool is the 2) <u>strategic business unit (SBU)</u>. With this approach, it is possible to see the individual 3) <u>contribution</u> that each product makes to the overall company profitability.

A further useful tool is the idea of the 4) <u>break-even point</u>. Using this tool, prices may be raised or cut, but with a proper understanding of the effect.

Businesses should also make sure that there is a continually low level of 5) <u>inventory</u>.

Holding components or finished products is a waste of resources. It is better to operate a 6) <u>just-in-time (JIT)</u> approach. Storage is therefore kept to a minimum.

Control operations should focus on quality, service, efficiency and effective evaluation of the processes involved. There are three kinds of operational control: 7) <u>precontrol</u>, 8) <u>concurrent control</u> and 9) <u>postcontrol</u>.

The benefits of good operational control are shown in terms of increased profit and long term security for the business.

a	a focus on the quality of inputs in the production process
b	analysis of each separate product as a separate cost centre
c	goods in storage
d	gross profit margin
e	planning, controlling and monitoring all the activities of the business, so that efficiency is maintained, waste is cut to a minimum, quality is enhanced, customer satisfaction improves and profitability goes up.
f	policy of taking delivery of goods only when they can be used, and producing to order
g	monitoring quality after the production or output of service
h	evaluation of the conversion of inputs to outputs as it happens
i	demonstrating the volume required at a certain price to produce the required profit

1	2	3	4	5	6	7	8	9
e								

Pre-, *con-* and *post-* are all prefixes. *Pre-* usually indicates before; *con-* can sometimes indicate with or at the same time; *post-* usually means after. Another common prefix is *contra-* indicating against. Examples are *premature, precondition, pre-determined; contemporary, convention; postpone, postscript; contravention, contradict.*

24 Other aspects of profitability

Match the underlined phrases to similar phrases in the box.

> budgeted income statement   capital employed   current assets
> current liabilities   debtors   net income   stock
> turnover   work-in-progress

A   Two documents provide the necessary information for the most important decisions about the strength of a business: a (1) <u>forecast profit and loss account</u> and the present balance sheet.

B   A study of profitability must look at the relationship between:

- (2) <u>income after all costs have been deducted</u> and (3) <u>total invoiced sales</u>;

- net income and the amount of (4) <u>money invested in the business</u>.

C   A study of a company's ability to make enough cash should show:

- if the planned cash balance is satisfactory;

- if (5) <u>people who owe money</u> are likely to pay on time;

- (6) <u>work which has been contracted but not yet invoiced</u> or (7) <u>finished goods</u> which will one day be sold;

- if the relationship between fixed assets and (8) <u>cash or other items of value which can easily be converted into cash</u> is satisfactory;

- if the relationship between current assets and (9) <u>debts due for payment</u> is satisfactory, i.e. current assets should be much greater than liabilities.

Management should be careful with forecasts, because budgeting is not a science and forecasts cannot be exact.

Businesses often fail because of problems of **liquidity**: they cannot meet their **short-term cash** needs.

25 Key terms in measuring financial performance 1

The phrases on the left are commonly used in considerations of the financial strength of a company. Match each one to an appropriate explanation on the right. Use the grid below.

1	company accounts	a	The description of income and expenditure in a specific accounting period.
2	profit and loss account	b	Items of value which are not easily changed into cash but which the business needs.
3	balance sheet	c	Documents showing income, expenditure, assets and liabilities, sales records, etc.
4	opening balance	d	Major spending on large items necessary for the business, such as property or equipment.
5	closing balance	e	Cash items, or items that can easily be changed into cash for the present financial year.
6	capital expenditure	f	The amount of money held in cash or near cash at the end of the accounting period.
7	fixed assets	g	The cost of borrowing from a bank.
8	current assets	h	Money made by the company, less all costs, but before tax has been paid.
9	net sales	i	The amount of money held in cash or near cash at the start of the accounting period.
10	pre-tax profit	j	The overall picture of assets and liabilities.
11	interest paid	k	The profit from sales after direct costs have been deducted.

1	2	3	4	5	6	7	8	9	10	11
c										

Note the verbs to **borrow** and to **lend**. A bank lends money. That is a **loan**. A **borrower** borrows a loan. But, there is also the less common verb to loan. This is a more formal word, meaning the same as to make a loan or to lend. Example: *The bank loaned the company $500,000.*

26 Key terms in measuring financial performance 2

Change the underlined words or phrases in the sentences below to other words or phrases that have a similar meaning. Choose from the box.

> abbreviated accounts   capital investment   consolidated
>
> debts equity   extraordinary items   gross   liquid assets
>
> operating income   revenue

1   <u>Unpredictable and exceptional costs</u> should be a separate item in the financial report.

2   The <u>trading income</u> needs to increase each year so that the company can make <u>decisions to buy new plant and equipment</u>.

3   The company accounts have been <u>checked and approved by an independent financial expert</u>.

4   Shareholders expect to see the <u>short description of the company's financial position</u>.

5   <u>Income</u> during the present tax year is less than last year.

6   <u>Pre-tax</u> earnings are down.

7   The <u>total value</u> of a company once all <u>liabilities</u> have been paid.

8   A successful company needs <u>property and investments that can be easily converted into cash</u>.

- Notice the pronunciation of *debt* /dɛt/. The *b* is silent. The same happens with **debtor** (someone who owes money). Another common word with a silent letter is *mortgage*, where the *t* is silent. A **mortgage** is a loan taken out to buy property, or to raise money against the value of property.

- The word **plant** is used for heavy machinery, especially in the construction industry, but also in other sectors of manufacturing.

27 The balance sheet

Match the words or phrases on the left with the correct definition (a-i). Use the grid below.

1	intangible assets	a	The money paid to shareholders out of profits.
2	fixed assets	b	Regular costs and money owed.
3	liquidity	c	Any investments, cheques, bank deposits, stock or work-in-progress that can easily be converted into cash.
4	depreciation	d	Assets which can be used to make immediate payments.
5	current assets	e	Property, land and equipment which is not normally intended for immediate sale.
6	dividend	f	Brand names, patents, rights, trade marks and licences which may be the major part of a company's wealth.
7	liabilities	g	The total amount borrowed from a bank.
8	liquid assets	h	The ability of a company to pay suppliers, employees, shareholders, tax authorities, etc.
9	overdraft	i	The notional fall in value of equipment over time.

1	2	3	4	5	6	7	8	9
f								

Depreciation is calculated by dividing the purchase price of an item of **capital expenditure** (usually a machine or vehicle, for example) by the useful life of the item, for example four years. Then that 25% of the purchase cost is treated as an **expenditure** in each of four years in the company accounts.

28 Reading a balance sheet

Look at this example of a balance sheet. Replace the underlined words or phrases with a word or phrase from the box with a similar meaning.

> bank overdraft   capital reserves   creditors   land   ordinary shares
> plant   preference shares   share capital   stock   tax   working capital

---

BOGUS INDUSTRIES plc

Balance sheet as at 31 December 2001

	$000	
ASSETS		
Fixed assets		
(1) <u>Property</u>	420	
Buildings	180	
(2) <u>Equipment</u> and machinery	100	
Total fixed assets		**700**
Current assets		
Raw materials		
Work-in-progress (3) <u>goods held in storage</u>	200	
Finished goods		
Debtors	90	
Cash in bank	60	
Total current assets		**350**
Current liabilities		
(4) <u>People owed money</u>	80	
(5) <u>Money owed to the bank</u>	50	
(6) <u>Money owed to the government</u>	35	
Total current liabilities		**165**
(7) <u>Net current assets</u>		**185**
Net assets		**885**
CAPITAL		
(8) <u>Money invested in the company and represented by shares</u>		
(9) <u>Shares paying a variable dividend to shareholders</u>	500	
(10) <u>Shares paying a fixed dividend to shareholders</u>	300	
(11) <u>Shares held in a special fund used to pay off creditors if the company goes into liquidation</u>	85	
Total		**885**

---

29 Reading a profit and loss account

Fill in the missing words (1–7). Choose from the following:

> cost of sales   depreciation   expenses   gross profit margin
> overheads   pre-tax profit   ~~sales income~~

RBH plc
PROFIT AND LOSS ACCOUNT
for the year ending 31 December 2001

€000

(1) __*sales income*__		2,4650
(2) _____		
Materials	870	
Labour	790	
		1,660
(3) _____ (profit)		990
(4) _____		
Salaries	220	
Capital expenditure	120	
Distribution	140	
Advertising	85	
Administration	80	
Bank loans, interest payments	38	
(5) _____		
Rent	12	
Heat, light, telephone	11	
Miscellaneous	8	
(6) _____	55	
		769
(7) _____		221

Remember that **depreciation** shows loss of value in **capital equipment**. It is not a true cash expenditure, but is usually shown this way in profit and loss accounts.

30 Introducing key terms in banking

Complete the words below to match the given meanings.

1   The person to whom a cheque is written.   p a y e e

2   Money provided by a bank to a customer, for an
    agreed purpose.   l _ _ _

3   A bank which offers a full range of services
    to individuals and companies.   c _ m _ _ _ _ _ _ l b _ _ _

4   A type of bank with a strong local or regional
    identity, mainly used by small, private investors,
    who get interest on their deposits.   s _ _ _ _ _ _ b _ _ _

5   An instruction from one bank to another bank
    asking it to make a payment to a supplier.   _ _ _ k d _ _ _ _

6   An agreement that an account can remain in debit
    up to a certain amount for an agreed time period.   o _ _ _ _ _ _ _ _

7   The time taken from when a cheque is presented to
    a bank to when the receiving account is credited.   c _ _ _ r _ _ _ e

8   Fees charged by a bank for services provided.   _ _ n _ c _ _ _ _ s

9   An instruction from a customer to a bank to
    make a regular payment to a creditor. Instructions
    to alter the dates or the payments must come
    from the customer.   s _ _ _ _ _ _ g o _ _ _ r

10 A computer printout sent by a bank to a customer,
    showing recent activity on his/her account.   s _ _ _ _ _ _ _ t

11 The lowest level of interest that a bank
    charges for lending money.   b _ _ _ r _ _ _

12 Conducting banking services from a computer
    using the bank's website.   I _ _ _ _ _ _ t b _ _ _ _ _ _

A **payee** is someone who is paid. A **payer** pays someone else. A similar
contrast exists between **employee** and **employer** and between **franchisee**
and **franchiser**. Verbs exist in all these cases: **pay**, **employ** and **franchise**.

31 Banking and using money

Complete the sentences below with a word or phrase from the box.

> ~~bank draft~~   cash point   cheque book   debit card
> direct debit   electronic funds transfer (EFT)   home-banking   night safe
> paying-in slip   PIN number (personal identification number)
> standing order   statement   withdrawal receipt

1   If I want my bank to transfer money to another bank I ask for a
    bank draft .

2   A plastic card that I can use to pay for goods in shops that means that
    money is immediately transferred to the shop's bank is called a
    _____ .

3   Banks normally send out a _____ every month. It is a complete
    record of all transactions on the named account.

4   When someone pays cash or cheques into a bank, they complete a
    _____ .

5   If you need cash urgently, you can usually get some – even at night –
    from a _____ .

6   When you use your bank card to get cash, you have to know your
    _____ .

7   Most people who have a bank account can pay for goods and services by
    using a _____ , or if it is a regular payment, they may set up a
    _____ .

8   A _____ is an agreement to pay a creditor a sum of money on a
    regular basis, where the creditor can alter the dates or amounts of the
    payment.

9   Some banks operate a _____ facility where you can deposit cash.

10 If you take money from your account you normally get a _____ .

11 The instant movement of money from one account to another using
    computers and the telephone network is called _____ .

12 Carrying out simple banking operations such as checking your account,
    making transfers or payments from home, either by phone or using a
    computer is _____ .

American Express, VISA and Mastercard are **credit cards**. You pay at the
end of the month and so get up to one month's credit from the card issuer.
With a **debit card**, your account is debited immediately.

32 Banking services

A Credit Bank International offers the following services to customers planning to export to new markets. Divide the products into two categories: finance and services.

~~allowances against bills for collection~~	foreign currency loans and overdrafts
bank transfer	Internet banking
banker's order	letter of credit
buyer credit	standing order
economic information	status enquiries
foreign currency account	trade development advice

Finance	Services
allowances against bills for collection	_____
_____	_____
_____	_____
_____	_____
_____	_____
	_____
	_____

B Look at the following extracts from a flyer for Credit Bank International. Complete the spaces using appropriate services or products from the box in A.

CBI can help you develop an international business

Trading internationally

1 Our _____ service offers an up-to-date assessment of the political and economic prospects in particular countries or regions.

2 We also provide _____ which matches your company to a specific partner, either a customer or a supplier.

3 To make sure that your partner is reliable, we carry out _____, a check on their credit rating, to see if they have a good level of liquidity.

4 We offer finance to help your cashflow situation, using _____ . This means we provide a loan, and the money you are owed by a customer is a kind of security.

5 Or we lend money to your customer at fixed interest rates, so you get paid quickly. This is called _____ .

Foreign money

6 We also provide cash when you need it. We can set up _____. This is useful if you travel abroad a lot. This can be at fixed interest rates, so that you have no problems with changes in exchange rates.

7 We can also provide a _____, with cheque books, overdraft facilities, bank cards and cash whenever you need them, in the foreign currency.

Paying your supplier

8 The easy and safe way to pay a supplier abroad is through a _____ , though there are charges.

9 For regular business, payments can be made using a _____. This is an agreement where the buyer can draw on amounts up to an agreed limit for an agreed purpose. The buyer sends all the relevant documents to the supplier. The supplier then takes the documents to a local bank to get paid.

10 Another way to make regular payments is using a _____, which pays a regular amount that can only be changed if you tell the bank to change it.

11 The alternative, useful if the amount changes regularly, is a _____, where the creditor can change the amount paid, or the dates for payment.

Keeping in touch

12 CBI offers a comprehensive _____ service. You can access your account, check balances, transfer funds and make payments from anywhere in the world with a computer linked to the web. On-line banking allows you to stay in touch and keep control.

Internet banking and **on-line banking** mean the same thing.

33 Bank charges

Choose the best explanation for each of the terms in italics from a), b) or c).

1 *unauthorized overdraft fee*
   a) a special low rate of interest charged to customers who are in difficulty
   b) a higher rate of interest charged if an account is overdrawn above an agreed maximum
   c) a single penalty fee charged to an account if it is overdrawn above an agreed maximum

2 *setting-up fee*
   a) a charge made for a new account
   b) a charge when money is paid in or taken out from an account
   c) a fixed charge when an overdraft agreement is made

3 *base rates*
   a) the rate of interest charged to customers who borrow from the bank
   b) a rate used to help decide the level of interest on loans from the bank (The bank usually sets the actual interest rate several points above the base rate.)
   c) all charges made to an account in a year

4 *margin*
   a) the percentage above the base rate that a borrower is asked to pay
   b) the profit that a customer makes from having an account in credit and so earning interest
   c) the cost of borrowing

5 *fixed rate lending*
   a) an agreement to lend money at a current rate of interest that could change if base rates go up or down
   b) lending money at an agreed interest rate for a fixed time
   c) any agreement to lend money for a fixed period of time

6 *commission*
   a) a percentage of a credit or debit which may be deducted by the bank
   b) a request by a bank that more money should be paid into an account
   c) a bonus paid by the bank to a customer if charges have been too high

7 *handling charge*
   a) a special fee charged after a meeting with a customer
   b) a fee charged by the bank in relation to a particular payment
   c) a fee charged to an account for changing money from one currency to another

8 *interest*
   a) a percentage fee added to the debt you have with the bank if you are borrowing money
   b) a charge made by the bank on any account they provide
   c) a payment made to your account as a percentage of the amount you have deposited in the bank

9 *annual fee*
   a) typical charge for being a bank customer
   b) charge for using cash points from other banks
   c) charge for some types of credit card

10 *withdrawal fee*
   a) charge for closing your bank account
   b) charge for using a cash point to get money from your account
   c) charge for using internet banking

This test is about bank charges, but in fact many banking services are actually free. For example, a **current account**, if it remains in credit, is often a free service. The bank can in effect use your money to increase its **reserves**. It therefore is good for you (because it is free and convenient) and good for the bank. The bank may also sell you other services that are not free.

34 Planning borrowing

Organize the following into categories under the given headings, each of which would be discussed with the bank in negotiating support for a business venture.

> ability to pay   amount requested   assets   business plan
> capital needs   existing capital resources   experience
> ~~financial projections~~   insurance   loan period   marketing plan
> purpose of borrowing   realism of financial projections
> repayment method   security   skills   track record

Planning

financial projections

_____

_____

Business background

_____

_____

Financial strength

_____

_____

_____

Requirements

_____

_____

_____

Human resources

_____

Protection of loan

_____

Repayment

_____

_____

Banks support new business ideas if they can see the potential **benefits** of the new business for the people involved and for the bank. Banks typically want to see a **business plan**, setting out the marketing, financial and practical steps in starting up the new business. Banks are therefore important **stakeholders** in new and established businesses. Stakeholders are all those individuals and groups with a direct personal interest in the fortunes of the business, including employees, suppliers, customers, the local community and even the national economy in the case of large businesses.

35 Introducing key terms in insurance

Complete the words below to match the given meanings.

1 Payment made by an insurer. in d e mn i t y

2 A document which is evidence that someone has insurance.
i _ _ _ _ _ _ _ e c _ _ _ _ _ _ _ _ e

3 Covered by an insurance policy. i _ _ _ _ _ d

4 Possibility that something might happen. r _ _ _

5 The amount charged for insurance. p _ _ _ _ _ m

6 Payment to help someone who has suffered loss or injury.
c _ _ p_ _ s _ _ _ _ _

7 Insurance protection. c _ _ _ _

8 A small part of the total loss which should be paid by the insured person when he/she makes an insurance claim. e _ _ _ _ s

9 A type of insurance which pays out on the death of the insured, or at a specific pre-determined time. l _ _ _ a _ _ _ _ _ n _ _

10 A type of insurance to meet hospital costs due to illness or after an accident or injury. m _ _ _ _ _ l i _ _ _ _ _ _ _ e

11 A person whose job is to find appropriate insurance at an appropriate price. b _ _ _ _ _

12 A description of what happened and a request to an insurer to meet the costs resulting from the event. _ _ _ _m

13 Someone other than the insured who suffers loss or injury in an accident. t _ _ _ _ p _ _ _ _

14 A document issued by an insurance company describing the type of insurance offered and requesting payment. s _ _ _ _ _ _ e

15 A document describing an insurance agreement. p _ _ _ _ y

16 The period for which an insurance policy is effective. t _ _ _

Notice the verbs **claim** (from an insurance company or policy) and **claim damages against** someone. **Damages** here means compensation for harm or injury. *Damages* is a plural and uncountable word. Where *damage* is singular it means damage or harm to a thing (not a person). It is also uncountable.

Another meaning of *claim* is much more common and non-technical. This is to state that something is a fact, for example *The scientist claimed that chimpanzees think in a similar way to humans*. There is also the noun, *claim*. Example: *The claim was rejected by a local zoo keeper.*

36 An insurance claim

Antonio Alessandro has sent a claim form to his insurer after a fire at his restaurant. He receives the reply below. Complete the text with appropriate words from the box.

~~claim~~   compensation   comprehensive   cover
estimate   indemnity   legal costs   loss adjuster
no claims bonus   policy   premium

Bridge Insurance Ltd
124 Kew Gardens Road, London SW2 5HB
Tel: 0207 433 8211 Fax: 0207 433 5633

Antonio Alessandro
Ristorante Colosseo
120 Riverside Road
London EC23 5TR
2 March 2002

Dear Mr Alessandro
Re: Policy number DR 239981 R, Claim Ref. DR4381
Thank you for your (1)_____*claim*_____ relating to the fire at your restaurant. We confirm that your policy is (2)_____ and therefore covers fire.

Our (3)_____, Peter Carrow, will visit you on 7 March to see the damage.

You will receive (4)_____ for all damage to the building and equipment. You should supply an (5)_____ from two firms for the repairs. You will also receive (6)_____ for loss of business, though you will have to make a separate claim. In addition, your (7)_____ also provides (8)_____ for any (9)_____ which may arise.

Finally, we would like to inform you that your (10)_____ will rise by 10% as your (11)_____ will be affected by this incident.

Yours sincerely
Janina Piontek
Janina Piontek
Claims Manager

The normal conventions of greetings and farewells in letters are:
Dear Mr/Mrs/Ms Bailey (named addressee)   *Yours sincerely*
Dear Sir (unnamed addressee)   *Yours faithfully*
We normally use the name of the addressee if we know it.

37 Key terms in investment

A   Find 10 key words concerned with investments in the word square below.

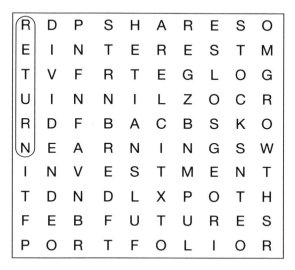

R	D	P	S	H	A	R	E	S	O
E	I	N	T	E	R	E	S	T	M
T	V	F	R	T	E	G	L	O	G
U	I	N	N	I	L	Z	O	C	R
R	D	F	B	A	C	B	S	K	O
N	E	A	R	N	I	N	G	S	W
I	N	V	E	S	T	M	E	N	T
T	D	N	D	L	X	P	O	T	H
F	E	B	F	U	T	U	R	E	S
P	O	R	T	F	O	L	I	O	R

B   Match a word in the square to one of the definitions below.

1   Spending or using money to make more money in the future

2   The total collection of shares, accounts, bonds, trusts, and other financial items that an individual owns

3   The profit from investments

4   A part ownership in a company represented by a piece of paper (a certificate). The value, or price, may rise or fall

5   Shares that will be paid for at a fixed price in the future, or an agreement to buy shares at a fixed price at some time in the future

Internet trading of stocks and shares has developed strongly in recent years. There are very many websites advising on investments, but many are not very reliable. People may post positive information on a particular company to websites to boost the company **share price,** and therefore boosting the profit of existing **shareholders.**

38 Making money work

It is well known that keeping your money under the bed is not the safest or most effective way of looking after it. Individuals and companies invest spare funds in order to make more money.

A Below are different investment choices. Mark them as H (high), M (medium) or L (low) risk. Remember high risk investments can make a lot of money, but they can also go wrong. Low risk investments usually make much less profit, but rarely go wrong.

1 Shares in new companies in developing markets $\boxed{H}$

2 Property investment in established and expensive locations ☐

3 Property investment in remote but beautiful places ☐

4 Government bonds ☐

5 High interest bank accounts ☐

6 Unit trusts in the USA and Europe ☐

7 Seed corn investment in new telecommunications, media and technology sector (TMT) ☐

8 Shares in top NASDAQ companies ☐

9 Unit trusts in developing markets ☐

10 Employee pension scheme ☐

11 Individual Savings Accounts (ISAs) ☐

B Choose the right explanation for 6 of the above from the alternatives below.

1 Seed corn investment is:

a) buying a new business
b) giving a large sum of money to help the start up of a new business and becoming a part owner or shareholder in the business
c) investing money at a fixed level of interest in a new business

2 NASDAQ is:

a) a share index of mainly high technology businesses on the New York Stock Exchange
b) a network of banks
c) a group of telecommunications companies in Japan

3 Unit Trusts are:

a) a group of investments in a range of different companies, sometimes restricted to a geographical region, or specific sector, or with a specific investment objective.
b) Government-managed investments in government-owned companies
c) Investments in top companies quoted on major world stock exchanges

4 Employee pension plans are:

a) private pensions that people in work set up independently
b) also known as occupational pension plans, where the employer and the employee pay into a fund which is invested to provide pensions for company staff
c) government pension scheme for people in work

5 Government bonds are:

a) fixed interest investments issued and guaranteed by the government
b) investments in currencies
c) investments in nationalized (state-owned) companies

6 ISAs are:

a) a bank account giving a high interest return
b) a share investment in different companies which is tax free (for UK residents)
c) a pension plan

Government bonds are also known as **gilt edged investments**, or **gilts**.
NASDAQ is an acronym for the National Association of Securities Dealers Automated Quotations.

39 Describing trends and share movements

A Rewrite the following sentences, beginning with the given words, and replacing the words in italics with a verb phrase.

1 There has been a *marked rise* in sales for Axal in recent weeks.

Axal sales *have risen markedly in recent weeks* _____

2 Frodo has suffered a *sudden drop* in market share.

Frodo's market share _____

3 Spino showed a *slight fall* in share price last week.

Spino's share price _____

4 There will be a *quick recovery* in the share price.

The share price will _____

5 A *levelling off* of sales for FDT is expected.

FDT sales _____

6 There has been a *considerable decline* in the market.

The market _____

7 There was a *sharp increase* in share prices.

Share prices _____

8 The *severe fluctuation* in share values was because of increasing evidence of a price war.

Share prices _____

9 HD experienced a *rapid rise* in market share in the late 1990s.

HD's market share _____

B Match each of the following phrases to an appropriate graph below showing recent share performance. Look at the line between the two crosses.

collapsed   edged down   fell back   firmed   rallied   steadied   stepped up

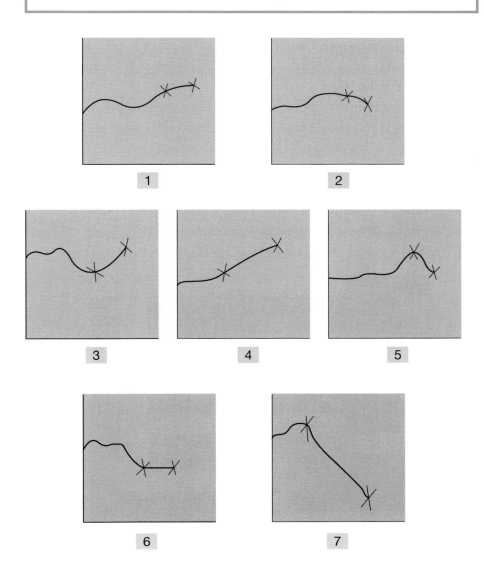

40 Stock exchanges

Complete the crossword below.

Across

1   The city which is the financial capital of Germany. (9)

5   Goods like coffee, tea, cocoa, metals and oil that are traded in large quantities. (11)

6   The index of share prices in the New York Stock Exchange. (3, 5)

7   An acronym for a company that has shares quoted on the UK Stock Exchange. (3)

9   A computer measurement of the share performance of 100 leading UK companies. (7)

10   A contract to buy shares at a fixed price in the future. (6)

11   A part of a company's total capital that can be bought and sold. (5)

Down

2   A method of raising capital by selling new shares to existing shareholders, usually at a discount. (6, 5)

3   A name commonly given to Footsie 100 companies. (4, 4)

4   A low risk investment issued by governments (4)

8   The place where stocks and shares are traded in Paris. (6)

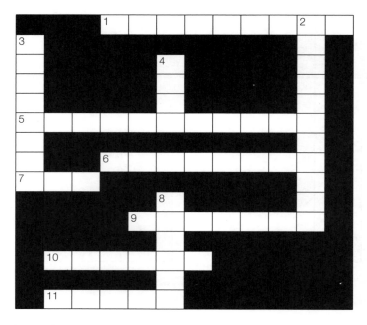

41 Market reports

The words in italics in the following sentences are commonly used to describe share movements. Divide them into three columns: Up, Down, Same.

1. Burlesque shares *peaked* at 450p.
2. After steady rises, Axam shares *levelled off* at 320p.
3. Harrow *ended higher*, up 10p.
4. AJL *fell back* 20p.
5. Roadman *added* 5p in busy trading.
6. Media shares *sank* on news of planned government regulation.
7. News Newspaper Group *dipped* 20p to 540.
8. By the close of trading, Harnley had *steadied* at 320p.
9. Most of the oil sector *improved* in a bullish market.
10. Dolman *ended lower* at 320, off 20p.
11. Following steady gains, Kornan Foods *firmed* at 196p.
12. Food companies were generally up, *gaining* on the back of improved retail forecasts.
13. *Bearish* output forecasts indicate *sliding* share prices in the coming weeks.

Up	Down	Same
peaked		

Bears and bulls

These terms are **stock market** jargon for people who are optimistic about shares (**bulls**) and pessimistic about shares (**bears**). A company's shares, a sector, or the whole market may look **bullish** (rising), or **bearish** (in decline). **Investors** may buy shares when they are bearish as they think the shares are over-sold. Others might sell when they think investors have become too bullish.

42 Managing a personal investment portfolio

Match the term on the left (1–11) with an appropriate definition on the right (a–k). Use the grid below.

1	financial planner	**a**	A kind of life assurance for a specific time period.
2	insurance	**b**	The most important thing.
3	investment	**c**	An area of the economy, e.g. oil, pharmaceuticals, consumer electronics.
4	stockbroker	**d**	How safe an investment is.
5	pension	**e**	A part ownership in a company, usually by having shares in it.
6	priority	**f**	Someone who advises on investments, such as mortgages, life assurance policies, insurance, etc.
7	portfolio	**g**	Any attempt to spend money so that you have more money in the future.
8	risk	**h**	A regular amount of money that you get when you stop working because of your age.
9	sector	**i**	The total collection of investments that an individual has.
10	stake	**j**	A type of investment which provides protection against accidents.
11	term insurance	**k**	Someone who buys and sells stocks and shares.

1	2	3	4	5	6	7	8	9	10	11
f										

A **day trader** buys and sells shares on a daily basis to create short-term profit or to minimize losses. The cost of **share dealing** has reduced dramatically because of telephone share dealing and **Internet trading**. A day trader does all his own research and makes his own investment decisions. Day trading is very **high risk**.

43 Measuring investment performance

An Independent Financial Adviser (IFA) is explaining some key terms. Match the questions to the correct answer.

1 What is turnover? ___c___

2 What is EPS – earnings per share? _____

3 How do you calculate the price/earnings ratio? _____

4 What is the PEG factor? _____

5 What is cashflow-per-share? _____

6 What does 'relative strength' mean? _____

7 What is the 'margin'? _____

8 What's ROCE – or return on capital employed? _____

9 What is 'gearing'? _____

---

a This is another measure of company profitability. It tells us how much profit the company makes from what it actually spends in order to trade. It is a percentage measurement, and a high percentage is a good indicator.

b This is the percentage of profit the company makes from its turnover. For example if the company has a turnover of $500 million and it makes a profit of $50 million, then that's 10%.

c This is the total volume of sales.

d This shows how the company's share price has performed in percentage terms compared with other companies.

e This is a simple measure of how much cash a company generates from its customers, relative to the total number of shares.

f This is calculated by dividing the annual net profit by the total number of ordinary shares.

g G is for Growth, so this means the forecast growth in earnings. You calculate this by dividing the PE ratio by the estimated future growth of EPS.

h This is the price of an ordinary share related to the earnings or EPS. Price divided by earnings gives you the price/earnings ratio.

i A simple explanation is that it is a figure which compares the total borrowings of a company (less liquid assets) with the total share capital, or all the money raised from shareholders. If the figure is high, that's not so good.

44 Collective funds

Complete the following sentences with words or phrases from the box.

~~collective funds~~	investment trusts	OEICS	redeemed	trade
	traded	transaction	trust law	unit trusts	

1 **Collective funds** are companies set up to invest capital for investors.

2 _____ are a type of mutual fund common in the UK and English-speaking countries. They have the advantage of spreading risk over several companies.

3 _____ is the legal framework which governs the management of private trusts.

4 Unit trust investments are easily _____ or turned into cash.

5 _____ have a share base which is constant – new investments buy existing shares, they do not create new shares.

6 Both mutual trusts and investment trusts usually have lower _____ costs than life assurance savings products and bonds.

7 _____ are open-ended investment companies.

8 OEICS are flexible and easy to _____ , having a single price for both selling and buying.

9 OEICS are _____ and marketed internationally.

 Collective funds are known as **mutual funds** in the United States. Initial (**front end**) charges for collective funds can be quite high in comparison with direct investments in **gilts**, **eurobonds** and **equities**. **Unit trusts/investment trusts** can hold international investments but are UK investment products. They cannot be marketed or sold internationally.

45 Planning for the future

A Match the type of investment (1–5) with the correct description (a–e).

1 Occupational Pension Plan

2 Personal Equity Plan

3 Individual Savings Account (ISA)

4 Tax Exempt Special Savings Account

5 Group Pension Plan

a
- pension scheme for employees
- flexible, easily moved; so good for people who may change jobs frequently
- the employee takes the plan to the new employer

b
- safe cash-based investments
- an old product – you cannot take out a new one now
- tax free interest
- operated by banks and building societies
- minimum 5 year investment

c
- tax advantages (e.g. tax free dividends)
- the money is invested on world stock exchanges over the coming years
- growth depends on the performance of stocks
- there is risk if the investments are in companies which perform badly

d
- run by companies investing part of their own money and part of the employee's salary
- linked to a person's final salary on retirement
- pensions can be increased by making additional voluntary contributions (AVCs)

e
- seven year plans
- wider investment terms than PEPs/TESSAs
- maximum investment per year of £7000
- replacement for PEPs/TESSAs

B Mark the following statements as True or False. If they are false, explain why.

		True	False
1	TESSA is a common acronym for Tax Exempt Special Savings Account.	✓	☐
2	PEP is a common acronym for Personal Equity Plan.	☐	☐
3	Additional Voluntary Contributions means you have to pay extra into the fund.	☐	☐
4	Retirement is when you stop working.	☐	☐
5	A short-term investment is when you plan to invest the money for many years.	☐	☐
6	Tax exempt means you have to pay tax on profits from the investment.	☐	☐
7	A reasonably safe investment means low risk.	☐	☐
8	Linked to final salary means the same salary as on retirement.	☐	☐
9	Occupational Pension Plans are paid for by employees and employers.	☐	☐
10	Personal Equity Plans are based on investments in the world markets.	☐	☐
11	TESSAs are a cash-based investment with banks and building societies.	☐	☐
12	PEPs are still available in the UK.	☐	☐
13	PEPs will mature over the coming years.	☐	☐

46 Key words in talking about company relationships

Match each of the words or phrases on the left to an appropriate definition (a–l). Use the grid below.

1 bid	**a**	A proportion of the total share capital of a company.
2 buyout	**b**	Buying a majority of the shares in a company, and so winning control over the company.
3 competitor	**c**	Joining together of the stock of two companies, so they become part of the same company.
4 divestiture	**d**	The total equity capital of a company, held by shareholders in the form of shares.
5 flotation	**e**	An offer to buy part of the share capital of a company.
6 joint venture	**f**	A company which owns more than 50% of the shares in another company.
7 merger	**g**	The relationship between two companies, both owned by the same parent company.
8 parent company	**h**	Selling equity capital in a company, and so ending ownership of the company.
9 stake	**i**	A situation where workers or management buy all the equity (or more than 50%), or buy other assets, and so gain control of a business.
10 sister company	**j**	A business which is trying to sell in the same market as another business.
11 stock	**k**	An offer of sale to private investors of shares in a company backed by a prospectus on the stock exchange.
12 take-over	**l**	A temporary arrangement where two companies work together for a particular project.

1	2	3	4	5	6	7	8	9	10	11	12
e											

 A **prospectus**, published at the time of a **flotation**, describes the company and the **share offer** to possible **investors**.

47 Competitive tendering and joint bids

Read the following definitions and match them to words in bold in the advertisement below.

1 A group of companies who work together only for a particular contract.

consortium

2 A company owned and run by two or more people who do not receive interest on capital invested in the company.

_____

3 A company which is 100% owned by a parent company.

_____

4 A project with two or more partners.

_____

5 Someone brought in to work on part of a large project.

_____

6 A formal proposal to do something at a certain price in a certain time period.

_____

Puertos Secos S.A.
CALL FOR BIDS

Puertos Secos S.A. (the sponsor) invite offers for the operation of a dry port facility at Barajas, Madrid.

Tenders will be accepted from any **partnership**, private company, or consortium, including companies operating with **wholly-owned subsidiaries**, or **partially-owned subsidiaries**, or other **joint-venture agreements**. The use of **sub-contractors** is acceptable.

However the contract will be awarded to a single individual or company who shall be responsible for the management of the project.

Details from:
Ministerio de Asuntos Interiores, Departamento de Transportes,
c/Bernardino Obregón, 44-48, 28012 MADRID. Tel: (9) 1 530 09 06

---

48 Company strength and market position

Complete the words below to match the given meanings.

1   To grow, to get bigger.   <u>e</u> x <u>pa</u> n d

2   To stop activities that do not make much money and to reduce the number of staff.   r _ t _ _ _ _ l _ _ _

3   The action of winning ownership and control of another company.   _ _ q _ _ _ _ _ _ _ n

4   To join two companies to create one bigger company.   _ m _ _ g _ _ _ t _

5   A company that is owned by a parent company.   s _ _ s _ _ _ _ _ _

6   One company taking control of another, smaller one.   t _ _ _ – o _ _ _

7   Where one company is the only supplier to a particular market.   m _ _ _ p _ _ _

8   Where a parent company sells a subsidiary (the opposite of number 3 above).   d _ v _ _ t _ _ _ _ _

9   A large group, owning and controlling many companies.   h _ _ _ _ _ g c _ _ _ _ _ y

10   An illegal agreement between two or more companies to fix high prices.   c _ _ t _ _

11   Fixing low prices until a competitor goes out of business.   p _ _ _ _ w _ _

12   Two companies joining together to create one company.   m _ _ _ _ _

13   A de-merger, two companies separate.   b _ _ _ _ – u _

Notice the difference in meaning between the verbs *take over* and *overtake*.
Take over: obtain or assume control of something, or gain control of something from somebody else
Overtake: to catch up with and pass a person, a vehicle travelling in the same direction or a competitor
A **takeover** (notice spelling of noun) is generally a hostile merger where the company taking control of another does so against its wishes. A **merger** is usually a common decision, welcomed by both parties.

49 Miscellaneous word phrases

The words in this test relate to different aspects of trading and investment in an international business environment. Complete the phrases with an appropriate word from the box below.

~~black~~	bonus	break	bridging	intangible	interim	issue
	line	loss	red	reserves	retail	securities

1 The part of an economy which is not declared to the tax authorities is known as the ___*black*___ economy.

2 A business that is losing money is running at a _____ .

3 A bank account that is in deficit is in the _____ .

4 Free shares given to long-term shareholders are called _____ shares.

5 If a business will meet its costs but not make any profit, it will _____ even.

6 If you want to buy something quickly you can borrow money on your assets by taking out a _____ loan. You pay back the loan after you sell some assets.

7 The final return on a business deal, indicating whether the deal made a profit or not, is sometimes called the bottom _____ .

8 A measure of prices paid in the shops is the _____ price index.

9 The payment to shareholders at the half-year point is called the _____ dividend.

10 The price of shares when a company is first floated on the Stock Exchange is called the _____ price.

11 Large amounts of foreign currency held by a company, bank or government, as a security against changes in exchange rates, are called foreign currency _____ .

12 Stocks and shares held by governments are called government _____ .

13 Assets which have a value but cannot be seen, e.g. customer goodwill, patents or trade marks, are called _____ assets.

The **retail price index** is known as the **consumer price index** in the United States. **Intangible assets** are also known as **invisible assets**.

50 Deregulating markets

A Complete the table with the correct form of the given words.

Verb	Agent	General noun	Adjective
	–	monopoly	
	competitor		
deregulate	–		
	–		authorized
	legislator		
		protection	
nationalize	–		
	regulator		
		partnership	–
	trader		traded/trading
	–		subsidized

B Use appropriate forms of these words to complete the text.

BT TO GAIN FROM EU COMPETITION LAWS

British Telecom is going to attack the (1) _____ position of its German (2) _____ Deutsche Telekom. BT wants a (3) _____ with two German competitors, RWE and Viag. The EU is trying to (4) _____ the European telecoms industry.

The EU wants to increase competition and open up (5) _____ across frontiers. In France, for example, France Telecom is in a strongly (6) _____ domestic market. The company is also (7) _____ by the government.

51 Financial problems

The text below is about a company in difficulty. First read the short text, then choose the best explanation for each term given below.

Sam Air Grounded

Sam Air is going to call in the receivers. The aircraft company does not have a serious bidder, after inviting partners to join a restructuring plan.

Sam Air's major creditor, Credit Bank International, refused to reschedule payments and has called in the debt. The company will probably go into liquidation soon. A rights issue failed three years ago when shareholders refused to put in more capital.

1 receivers
   a) directors of a company
   b) accountants who close down a company and give its assets to creditors and shareholders
   c) shareholders who receive the assets of a company that stops trading

2 restructuring
   a) reorganization of how the company is run
   b) reducing company costs by cutting the work-force
   c) reorganizing the ownership of equity capital and the way debts are financed

3 to reschedule payments
   a) to increase the amount of interest
   b) to change the terms for paying back a loan
   c) to ask for a loan to be taken over by another lender

4   to call in a debt
   a)   to ask a creditor to pay what is owed
   b)   to increase interest payments on a debt
   c)   to agree to late payment of a debt

5   go into liquidation
   a)   stop trading and have all assets given to creditors and shareholders
   b)   be declared bankrupt
   c)   change the type of activity of the business

6   rights issue
   a)   an attempt to enter new markets
   b)   an attempt to change the company into a workers' co-operative
   c)   a way of getting extra money into a company by selling shares to existing shareholders at a low price.

Businesses go bankrupt because they have **liquidity** problems or because they have problems relating to **marketing**. This could be that they do not produce goods or services that customers want at a competitive price. If businesses fail, usually the **assets** of the company are taken over by **receivers**. They are responsible for disposing of the assets and paying off **creditors**. **Shareholders** only receive what is left after creditors have been paid off.

52 Understanding news stories

Below are headings from newspaper reports on the business environment. Choose the best explanation of the keywords from a), b), or c).

US growth hits new high

1 Growth means:
- (a) increased gross domestic product (GDP), or the increase in total sales revenue
- b) improved exports for the US economy
- c) increased value of companies on the New York Stock Exchange

Consumer confidence down in Germany

2 Consumer confidence means:
- a) what people think about German industry
- b) what people think of their personal economic situation
- c) what shop owners think of business prospects

Japan's trade surplus falls

3 Trade surplus means:
- a) the positive balance in exports over imports
- b) the value of sales
- c) the share value of the top 100 Japanese companies

Tokai bank writes off Yen 8bn in bad debts

4 To write off debts means:
- a) get the money back from creditors
- b) forget the money, since the loans are not going to be paid back
- c) demand the money back immediately

Cleveland Best Inc. announces de-merger

5 A de-merger is:
- a) a temporary division
- b) a decision to split a company into two parts
- c) a return to two separate entities following a period as one company

Ireland's trade deficit with Germany smaller

6 A trade deficit is:
- a) where exports are larger than imports
- b) a positive balance in favour of sales over debts
- c) where the value of imports is greater than the value of exports

Oil industry confidence hit by over capacity and oil price slump

7 Over capacity means:
a) the industry is not producing enough to meet demand
b) production facilities are not working to their potential
c) supply is greater than demand

Italian chemical conglomerate to break up

8 A conglomerate is:
a) a large manufacturing company
b) a multinational company
c) a large holding company with many subsidiaries

Worldwide PC sales soar 70%

9 To soar means:
a) increase by a large amount
b) go up a little
c) fall dramatically

Corporate phone bills to fall

10 Corporate means:
a) large
b) big business
c) personal, domestic and business

Worldwide corporate tax hits 40%

11 Corporate tax means:
a) special rate of tax on companies with large turnovers
b) taxes on any business activity
c) taxes on everyone, private individuals and companies

James Inc. makes $2bn from home entertainments sell-off

12 A sell-off is:
a) a successful sales campaign
b) a special promotion of low price goods
c) a decision to sell a subsidiary in an industrial group

- **Corporate tax** is also called **corporation tax**, especially in the UK.
- The word *entertainment* is normally uncountable, and therefore always takes a singular verb. In the example above, *home entertainments* is a short form of the noun phrase *home entertainment product sector*.

53 Key economic terms

Match the words on the left with the correct definition (a–l). Use the grid below.

1	central bank	a	Education and skills development for young people and the unemployed.
2	exchange rate	b	The part of the economy that does not make goods, also known as the tertiary sector.
3	inflation	c	The money a government needs to borrow to pay for what it does.
4	interest rates	d	The value of a currency against other currencies.
5	invisible earnings	e	The annual cost of borrowing money from a bank.
6	manufacturing industry	f	A measure of retail price increases.
7	national debt	g	The principal national banking authority.
8	public sector borrowing requirement	h	The part of the economy that makes products and changes raw materials into products.
9	public spending	i	The number, or percentage, of people out of work.
10	service sector	j	Government spending.
11	training	k	The total amount of money that a government owes.
12	unemployment rate	l	Income in foreign currency for services such as banking, insurance, tourism.

1	2	3	4	5	6	7	8	9	10	11	12
g											

The **European Central Bank** is, of course, not a national bank, but the supreme banking authority of the participating states in the euro (€) area within the European Union. It is based in Frankfurt.

54 Acronyms and abbreviations

Complete what the following stand for.

1 IMF   I _nternational_ Monetary F _und_

2 OPEC   O _ _ _ _ _ _ _ _ _ _ _ of Petroleum E _ _ _ _ _ _ _ _
Countries

3 PSBR   P _ _ _ _ _ S _ _ _ _ _ Borrowing Requirement

4 WTO   World T _ _ _ _ O _ _ _ _ _ _ _ _ _ _ _

5 EU   E _ _ _ _ _ _ _ _ U _ _ _ _

6 GNP   Gross N _ _ _ _ _ _ _ P _ _ _ _ _ _

7 OECD   O _ _ _ _ _ _ _ _ _ _ _ for E _ _ _ _ _ _ _ Co-operation
and Development

8 ASEAN   A _ _ _ _ _ _ _ _ _ _ of South East A _ _ _ _
N _ _ _ _ _ _

9 IBRD   International B _ _ _ for Reconstruction and
D _ _ _ _ _ _ _ _ _ _

10 WWF   World W _ _ _ _ _ _ _ Fund

11 UN   U _ _ _ _ _ N _ _ _ _ _ _

12 WHO   W _ _ _ _ Health O _ _ _ _ _ _ _ _ _ _

13 ECB   E _ _ _ _ _ _ _ C _ _ _ _ _ _ B _ _ _

14 NAFTA   N _ _ _ _ A _ _ _ _ _ _ _ Free T _ _ _ _ Agreement

15 MNCs   Multin _ _ _ _ _ _ _ C _ _ _ _ _ _ _ _ _ _ s

Gross Domestic Product (GDP) is based on the total value of all transactions within state borders. It is the sum of all invoiced goods and services. Governments produce such figures from tax returns. **Gross National Product (GNP)** includes returns from subsidiaries overseas where profits are repatriated.

55 Economic indicators

Mark the following sentences as True or False. If they are false, explain why.

		True	False
1	Inflation is a measure of increasing prices.	✓	
2	High inflation generally means increasing unemployment.		
3	A healthy consumer economy always means lower unemployment.		
4	Higher investment in training and education is easier during a low point in the economic cycle.		
5	A tight fiscal policy means high taxation and high government spending.		
6	Governments need to control their borrowing requirement.		
7	A high value of the local currency is good for exports.		
8	Housebuilding is seen as a good indicator of what is happening in the domestic economy.		
9	Gross national product (GNP) is a measure of the annual value of sales of goods and services in a country, and it does not include sales for companies abroad.		
10	Capacity utilization is a measure of how many people are in work.		

11	Generally, high levels of supply and low levels of demand means unemployment falls.	☐	☐
12	Growth creates wealth and wealth creates jobs.	☐	☐
13	Rationalization means cutting labour costs so people lose their jobs.	☐	☐
14	Increased investment in real terms means increased investment above inflation rates.	☐	☐
15	A balance of payments deficit means a company is spending more than it earns.	☐	☐
16	Fluctuations in exchange rates do not trouble financial planning.	☐	☐
17	If inflation is rising, a central bank will probably raise interest rates.	☐	☐
18	Stable and low inflation and interest rates are an economic 'good thing'.	☐	☐
19	High government spending can help to control inflation.	☐	☐
20	High labour mobility is generally good for an economy.	☐	☐

56 Managing the economy

Here are six newspaper headlines. Below them are the first lines of six articles. Match the headline to the right article.

1 MNCs will cut inward investment

2 RETAIL SALES UP – GOOD NEWS FOR JOBS

3 CALL FOR INVESTMENT IN TRAINING

4 REFLATION WOULD HELP HOUSEBUILDING, SAYS TOP OFFICIAL

5 INFLATION TARGET STILL 3%

6 HIGHER TAXES DESTROY POTENTIAL FOR GROWTH

7 CALL FOR DEVALUATION

a The Prime Minister has said again that retail prices must not rise above present levels. Speaking at a party meeting, he said low inflation was essential for economic recovery.

b An industrial pressure group has reported that the strength of the pound is damaging exports. The National Association of Exporting Industries recommends that the Government should devalue the pound by 10–12%. Exports have fallen by 5% as the pound has risen against all major currencies ...

c A report published this week claims that the increase in consumer spending is creating new employment opportunities.

d The depressed construction industry would benefit if the Government increased public spending and lowered taxes, according to ...

e The Government should spend more on training grants for young people and the unemployed, according to Jaqueline Ross, the region's Local Education Officer. This would bring long-term economic benefits ...

f The Minister of State for Finance, Peter Bluff, said yesterday that tax increases would be bad for industry. 'The best industrialists would leave the country and the damage to the national economy could be massive,' Mr Bluff said.

g A leading Japanese economist has suggested that multinational corporations will be less likely to invest in the UK if the pound continues to have such a high exchange rate against the euro.

- **Public spending** is another way of saying **government spending**. Government provides various **services**: health, social welfare, education, transport, and defence, for example. All these together are paid for from **taxation** and other forms of **government revenue**.
- **Consumer spending** is what people spend on goods and services.

57 Economic performance

The sentences below are extracts from a newspaper report on economic performance. Choose the correct explanation for the words in italics from a), b), or c).

1 *Retail sales* continued to grow in March, confirming the trend begun in the pre-Christmas boom, according to Paul Figg, of IMA Consultants.
   a) sales in the shops
   b) sales of clothes
   c) factory prices

2 Consumer demand will help *economic growth*, forecast at 4% for the year.
   a) price rises
   b) jobs
   c) total national income

3 Higher consumption of imported goods could result in a worsening *trade deficit*.
   a) decline in trade
   b) negative balance of value of exports and imports
   c) inflation

4 Uncertainty in the industrial job market is creating a lack of *consumer confidence*.
   a) employment in manufacturing
   b) spending in the shops
   c) feel-good factor in ordinary people

5 *Manufacturing output* is lower and exports have almost halved.
   a) building new factories
   b) industrial production
   c) employment in factories

6 There is a problem of excessive *stock levels* which means there are no new jobs.
   a) goods waiting to be sold
   b) strikes
   c) high prices

7 There is an economic slowdown in most major *export markets*.
   a) countries which normally export to this country.
   b) countries which normally buy from us.
   c) stock exchanges

58 Managing exchange rates

The sentences below describe how different economic factors affect each other. Complete the spaces with words or phrases from the box.

> balance of payments   ~~building societies~~   consumer spending   deficit
> exchange rates   exports   interest rates   unemployment

When banks and (1) _building societies_ offer credit, or cheap loans at low (2) _____ , consumer spending rises and (3) _____ go up. High (4) _____ creates pressure to increase wages. High consumer spending also creates more demand for imports. This causes problems for the (5) _____ . Imports also cost more when the exchange rate is high.

A high exchange rate also means lower (6) _____ .

Together these factors can make a worse balance of payments (7) _____ and higher inflation.

Higher inflation usually leads to higher (8) _____ .

Some building societies still exist in the UK. They are **mutual societies**, or **co-operatives** owned by the members and run for their benefit. They offer **mortgages** and other financial services to people buying their homes. In the late 1990s, many converted to banks and became PLCs, in effect owned not by their members, but by **shareholders**.

59 Central banks and economic stability

Choose the correct phrase from the alternatives in italics to create eight true sentences about economic management.

1   Most people think ~~politicians~~/ *bankers* are better than *politicians / ~~bankers~~* at running an economy.

2   Independent central banks have a good record on controlling *inflation / public opinion.*

3   Freedom to control *monetary policy/ banking regulations* means being able to change *exchange rates / political opinion.*

4   *Low interest rates / high interest rates* help to control *inflation / small banks.*

5   High interests rates often cause *small banks / central banks* to fail.

6   In developing countries, central banks cannot help small banks because of the risk of *low inflation / hyper-inflation.*

7   Newly independent central banks are limited by their agreements with the *International Monetary Fund / the United Nations.*

8   Any risk of inflation can mean *disinvestment /new investment* on the part of investment *fundholders /national governments.*

9   If an economy is experiencing major falls in the price of goods and a lack of demand, as well as falling employment, this is called *a recession / stagflation.*

- National economies are controlled by central banks, governments, and international financial interests. Economies are also affected by investment decisions by large private companies, multinational corporations, trade agreements, exchange rates, currency speculators, and the state of the regional, national and international economy.

- The difference between **recession** and **stagflation** is the rapidly falling prices under stagflation. **Hyper-inflation** is extremely high levels of **inflation** (rising prices and wages).

60 Friedman is not dead and Keynes lives

Read the imaginary dialogue below. It is between two economists: Milton Friedman, who believes in leaving everything to market forces; and J.M. Keynes, who believes in partnership between the State and private capital. They are discussing the impact of the European Airbus project on the world airliner market. Fill in the spaces with appropriate words from the box.

> competition   competitor   consortium   economies
> export subsidies   free trade   market share   ~~monopoly~~
> resources   scale   subsidies   suppliers

Keynes: The Airbus project has been good for consumers. It has stopped Boeing having a (1) ___*monopoly*___ in the airliner market.

Friedman: In fact, Boeing already had a (2) _____ in McDonnell Douglas.

Keynes: Yes, it did. But the Airbus did lower prices due to the arrival of more (3) _____ .

Friedman: But the benefits of Airbus do not match the subsidy which the European taxpayer paid for. (4) _____ is the best way to run the global economy. It is cheaper than tariff barriers, import quotas and (5) _____ .

Keynes: I can't agree. The airliner industry has few companies. They can make (6) _____ of (7) _____ . This means low costs and real competition between (8) _____ . This is what happened between Boeing and Airbus. The Airbus (9) _____ with four countries, has built up (10) _____ . The benefit to the European economy has been more than the cost of the _____ .

Friedman: I am not sure. I think subsidies are a waste of (12) _____ .

Keynes: Well, I think I'll have a cup of tea. Will you join me?

Friedman: Only if it's free market tea.

Biographical details

Milton Friedman, economist, born New York, 1912.

John Maynard Keynes, economist, born Cambridge, UK, 1883–1946.

Answers

Test 1

1	e	5	c	9	f
2	h	6	d	10	g
3	a	7	i		
4	j	8	b		

Test 2

1	m	6	j	11	n
2	b	7	h	12	i
3	a	8	e	13	o
4	l	9	f	14	g
5	k	10	c	15	d

Test 3

	Verb	Personal noun	General noun	Adjective
1	to analyze	analyst	analysis	analytical
2	to compete	competitor	competition	competitive
3	to advise	advisor	advice	advisory/advisable
4	to merge	–	merger	merged
5	to industrialize	industrialist	industry	industrial
6	to trade	trader	trade	trading/traded
7	to export	exporter	export(s)	exporting/exported
8	to produce	producer	product	productive
9	to supply	supplier	supply	supplied
10	to consume	consumer	consumption	consuming
11	to guarantee	guarantor	guarantee	guaranteed
12	to credit	creditor	credit	credited
13	to debit	debtor	debit	debited
14	to earn	earner	earnings	earned
15	to invest	investor	investment	invested

Test 4

1 table
2 row
3 column
4 pie chart
5 segment
6 histogram/bar graph
7 vertical axis
8 horizontal axis
9 line graph
10 dotted line
11 solid line
12 broken line
13 curve
14 fluctuating line
15 undulating line

Test 5

1	d	4	b	7	f
2	e	5	h	8	i
3	a	6	g	9	c

Test 6

A

rise/fall
increase/decrease
go up/go down
climb/decline
shrink/expand
deteriorate/improve
get better/get worse
collapse/escalate
hit bottom/peak

B

1	g	4	e	7	f
2	d	5	b	8	i
3	a	6	c	9	h

Test 7

	Public limited company	Private limited company	Sole trader	Partnership	Co-operative
Single individual owns company		possibly	✓		
Two or more owners/ directors	✓	✓		✓	
Quoted on stock exchange	✓				
Workers run on the company					✓
Unlimited liability			✓	✓	
Limited liability	✓	✓			possibly
Owner is self-employed			✓	possibly	

Test 8

1	VAT	Value Added Tax
2	PLC	Public Limited Company
3	Ltd	Limited
4	& Co.	and Company
5	CWO	Cash With Order
6	COD	Cash On Delivery
7	c.i.f	cost, insurance, freight
8	PAYE	Pay-As-You-Earn (i.e. tax)
9	p/e	price/earnings ratio
10	P & L account	Profit and Loss account

Test 9

1 profitability
2 turnover
3 core activity
4 gross profit margin
5 setting-up costs
6 overheads
7 net profit margin
8 cost of sales
9 break-even point
10 selling costs

Test 10

fixed costs	variable costs
labour costs (2)	production costs (3)
storage costs (7)	advertising costs (1)
administrative costs (4)	distribution costs (5)
	selling costs (6)

Test 11

1 fixed costs
2 variable costs
3 manufacturing costs
4 selling costs
5 labour costs
6 operating costs
7 cost price
8 cost analysis
9 cost centre
10 cost of sales

Test 12

A

1 income
2 forecast
3 sheet
4 budget
5 turnover
6 fixed
7 variable
8 raw
9 capital
10 administrative
11 cash

B

a forecast
b spending
c income
d expenditure
e budget
f banker's order

Test 13

1 petty cash
2 hard cash
3 cashflow
4 cash on delivery
5 cash budget
6 cash advance
7 ready cash
8 cash settlement
9 cash price

Test 14
A   Report: 2, 1, 5, 4, 3
B   Memo: 4, 2, 5, 1, 3

Test 15
1 demand
2 margin
3 price-sensitive
4 has passed its sell-by-date
5 price cut
6 inelastic
7 annual sales
8 turnover

Test 16
A   1 b   3 d
     2 c   4 a

B   1 d   6 i
     2 f   7 e
     3 g   8 a
     4 c   9 b
     5 h

Test 17
1 sales revenue
2 variable costs
3 total
4 variable
5 fixed
6 fixed costs
7 unit contribution
8 elastic

Test 18
Services
electricity account
telephone

Insurance
professional indemnity insurance
employer's liability insurance

Property
rent
mortgage payments

Vehicles
car and van hire
car hire purchase agreements

Miscellaneous costs
books, newspapers
stationery and printing

Employee costs
salaries
employee National Insurance
contributions (NICs)

Administration
secretarial support

Professional fees
accountancy fees

Equipment
equipment, machinery
leasing of computers

Test 19
1 a)   5 b)   9 b)
2 b)   6 b)   10 b)
3 c)   7 c)
4 a)   8 a)

Test 20
1 e   3 f   5 a
2 c   4 b   6 d

Test 21
1 fixed costs
2 variable costs
3 total costs
4 sales revenue
5 break-even point
6 loss
7 profit

Test 22
1 margin
2 cost plus
3 market price
4 penetration strategy
5 marginal cost
6 discount
7 skimming strategy
8 competition

Test 23
1 e   4 i   7 a
2 b   5 c   8 h
3 d   6 f   9 g

Test 24
1 budgeted income statement
2 net income
3 turnover
4 capital employed
5 debtors
6 work-in-progress
7 stock
8 current assets
9 current liabilities

Test 25
1	c	5	f	9	k
2	a	6	d	10	h
3	j	7	b	11	g
4	i	8	e		

Test 26
1 extraordinary items
2 operating income, capital investment
3 consolidated
4 abbreviated accounts
5 revenue
6 gross
7 equity, debts
8 liquid assets

Test 27
1	f	4	i	7	b
2	e	5	c	8	d
3	h	6	a	9	g

Test 28
1 land
2 plant
3 stocks
4 creditors
5 bank overdraft
6 tax
7 working capital
8 share capital
9 ordinary shares
10 preference shares
11 capital reserves

Test 29
1 sales income
2 cost of sales
3 gross profit margin
4 expenses
5 overheads
6 depreciation
7 pre-tax profit

Test 30
1 payee
2 loan
3 commercial bank
4 savings bank
5 bank draft
6 overdraft
7 clearance
8 bank charges
9 standing order
10 statement
11 base rate
12 internet banking

Test 31
1 bank draft
2 debit card
3 statement
4 paying-in slip
5 cash point
6 PIN number (personal identification number)
7 chequebook, standing order
8 direct debit
9 night safe
10 withdrawal receipt
11 electronic funds transfer
12 home-banking

Test 32
A
Finance
allowances against bills for collection
buyer credit
foreign currency account
foreign currency loans and overdrafts
letter of credit

Services
bank transfer
banker's order
economic information
standing order
status enquiries
trade development advice
Internet banking

B
1 economic information
2 trade development advice
3 status enquiries
4 allowances against bills for collection
5 buyer credit
6 foreign currency loans and overdrafts
7 foreign currency account
8 bank transfer
9 letter of credit
10 standing order
11 banker's order
12 Internet banking

Test 33
1 c)
2 c)
3 b)
4 a)
5 b)
6 a)
7 b)
8 a) or c), but c) is not a charge
9 c)
10 b)

Test 34
Planning
financial projections
business plan
realism of financial projections

Business background
experience
track record
marketing plan

Financial strength
assets
security
existing capital resources

Requirements
capital needs
amount requested
period of loan
purpose of borrowing

Human resources
skills

Protection of loan
insurance

Repayment
repayment method
ability to pay

Test 35
1 indemnity
2 insurance certificate
3 insured
4 risk
5 premium
6 compensation
7 cover
8 excess
9 life assurance
10 medical insurance
11 broker
12 claim
13 third party
14 schedule
15 policy
16 term

Test 36
1 claim
2 comprehensive
3 loss adjuster
4 indemnity
5 estimate
6 compensation
7 policy
8 cover
9 legal costs
10 premium
11 no claims bonus

Test 37

A

```
R D P S H A R E S O
E I N T E R E S T M
T V F R T E G L O G
U I N N I L Z O C R
R D F B A C B S K O
N E A R N I N G S W
I N V E S T M E N T
T D N D L X P O T H
F E B F U T U R E S
P O R T F O L I O R
```

B

1 investments
2 portfolio
3 earnings or return
4 share(s)
5 futures

Test 38

1 Shares in new companies in developing markets H
2 Property investment in established and expensive locations L
3 Property investment in remote but beautiful places M
4 Government bonds L
5 High interest bank accounts L
6 Unit trusts in the USA and Europe M
7 Seed corn investment in new telecommunications, media and technology sector (TMT). H
8 Shares in top NASDAQ companies M/H
9 Unit trusts in developing markets M/H
10 Employee pension scheme L
11 ISAs (Individual Savings Accounts) L

B

1	b	3	a	5	a
2	a	4	b	6	b

Test 39

A

1 Axal sales have risen markedly in recent weeks
2 Frodo's market share has dropped suddenly.
3 Spino's share price fell slightly last week.
4 The share price will recover quickly.
5 FDT sales will/should level off.
6 The market has declined considerably.
7 Share prices increased sharply.
8 Share prices fluctuated severely because of increasing evidence of a price war.
9 HD's market share rose rapidly in the late 1990s.

B

1	firmed	5	fell back
2	edged down	6	steadied
3	rallied	7	collapsed
4	stepped up		

Test 40

Across	**Down**
1 Frankfurt	2 rights issue
5 commodities	3 blue chip
6 Dow Jones	4 bond
7 PLC	8 Bourse
9 Footsie	
10 future	
11 share	

Test 41

Up

peaked	improved
ended higher	firmed
added	gaining

Down

fell back	dipped
sank	ended lower
	bearish/sliding

Same

levelled off	steadied

Test 42
1 f	5 h	9 c
2 j	6 b	10 e
3 g	7 i	11 a
4 k	8 d	

Test 43
1 c	4 g	7 b
2 f	5 e	8 a
3 h	6 d	9 i

Test 44
1 collective funds
2 unit trusts
3 trust law
4 redeemed
5 investment trusts
6 transaction
7 OEICS
8 trade
9 traded

Test 45
A
1 d	4 b
2 c	5 a
3 e	

B
1 True
2 True
3 False. Voluntary means optional.
4 True
5 False. Short-term investment means only a short time.
6 False. Tax exempt means you pay no tax on profits from the investment.
7 True
8 False. Linked to final salary means a proportion of the final salary.
9 True
10 True
11 True
12 False. PEPs are frozen. New ones are not available.
13 True

Test 46
1 e	5 k	9 a
2 i	6 l	10 g
3 j	7 c	11 d
4 h	8 f	12 b

Test 47
1 consortium
2 partnership
3 wholly-owned subsidiary
4 joint-venture agreement
5 sub-contractor
6 tender

Test 48
1 expand
2 rationalize
3 acquisition
4 amalgamate
5 subsidiary
6 take-over
7 monopoly
8 divestiture
9 holding company
10 cartel
11 price war
12 merger
13 break up

Test 49
1 black
2 loss
3 red
4 shares
5 break
6 bridging
7 line
8 retail
9 interim
10 issue
11 reserves
12 securities
13 intangible

Test 50

Verb	Agent	General noun	Adjective
to monopolize	–	monopoly	monopolistic
to compete	competitor	competition	competitive
to deregulate	–	deregulation	deregulated/regulatory
to authorize	–	authority/ authorization	authorized
to legislate	legislator	legislation	legislative
to protect	protector	protection	protected/protective
to nationalize	–	nationalization	nationalized
to regulate	regulator	regulation	regulated/regulatory
to partner	partner	partnership	
to trade	trader	trade	traded/trading
to subsidize	–	subsidy	subsidized

B

1 monopoly
2 competitor
3 partnership
4 deregulate
5 trade/competition
6 regulated/protected
7 subsidized

Test 51

1	b)	3	b)	5	a)
2	c)	4	a)	6	c)

Test 52

1	a)	5	c)	9	a)
2	b)	6	c)	10	b)
3	a)	7	b)	11	a)
4	b)	8	c)	12	c)

Test 53

1	g)	5	l)	9	j)
2	d)	6	h)	10	b)
3	f)	7	k)	11	a)
4	e)	8	c)	12	i)

Test 54

1 International Monetary Fund
2 Organization of Petroleum Exporting Countries
3 Public Sector Borrowing Requirement
4 World Trade Organization
5 European Union
6 Gross National Product
7 Organization for Economic Co-operation and Development
8 Association of South East Asian Nations
9 International Bank for Reconstruction and Development (World Bank)
10 World Wildlife Fund
11 United Nations
12 World Health Organization
13 European Central Bank
14 North American Free Trade Agreement
15 Multinational Corporations

Test 55

1 True
2 True
3 False. Not always. If consumption is high there may be more jobs in some sectors of the economy, such as retailing. However, if consumers are buying a lot of imported goods, there may be negative consequences and redundancies for domestic maufacturing.
4 False. It is most necessary during a downturn, but paying for it is more difficult for a government when income from taxation is down, and more difficult for private industry when income from sales is down.
5 False. The opposite: low taxation and low government spending.
6 True
7 False. It makes products more expensive, so less attractive, for importers.
8 True
9 False. This is gross domestic product (GDP). GNP includes companies abroad.
10 False. This is a measure of how much an industry is working to its full potential. If a company is producing only half the products that it is physically capable of producing, its capacity utilization is only 50%. This means redundancies are possible.
11 False. No. Unemployment normally rises in this case.
12 True. Generally true, but in an age of high technology, some sectors can experience high growth without creating much employment.
13 True
14 True
15 False. The term is used to describe government spending (where government is acting on behalf of the national economy), not company spending.
16 False. Financial planning needs stability in all areas, including currency values.
17 True
18 True
19 False. Low government spending helps control inflation.
20 True

Test 56

1 g	5 a
2 c	6 f
3 e	7 b
4 d	

Test 57

1 a	5 b
2 c	6 a
3 b	7 b
4 c	

Test 58

1 building societies
2 interest rates
3 exchange rates
4 consumer spending
5 balance of payments
6 exports
7 deficit
8 unemployment

Test 59

1 bankers, politicians
2 inflation
3 monetary policy, exchange rates
4 high interest rates, inflation
5 small banks
6 hyper-inflation
7 the International Monetary Fund
8 disinvestment, investment fundholders
9 stagflation

Test 60

1 monopoly
2 competitor
3 competition
4 free trade
5 export subsidies
6 economies
7 scale
8 suppliers
9 consortium
10 market share
11 subsidy
12 resources

Word list

The numbers after the entries are the tests in which they appear.